COVER COVER

Bible Study

7 Sessions for Homegroup and Personal Use

GW00360019

Revelation 1-3

Christ's call to the Church

John Houghton

Published 2008 by CWR, Waverley Abbey House, Waverley Lane, Farnham, Surrey GU9 8EP, UK. Registered Charity No. 294387. Registered Limited Company No. 1990308.

See back of book for list of National Distributors.

Unless otherwise indicated, all Scripture references are from the Holy Bible: New International Version (NIV), copyright © 1973, 1978, 1984 by the International Bible Society.

Concept development, editing, design and production by CWR

Cover image: Stock.xchng

Printed in England by Yeomans Press

ISBN: 978-1-85345-461-5

Contents

Introduction

You are guaranteed to be blessed as you read, hear and take to heart the book of Revelation! With its dramatic imagery and powerful symbolism, this amazing prophecy has a power over the mind, heart and imagination like no other. Its words have shaped everything from world history to Hollywood movies. They have also excited considerable controversy thanks to novel interpretations that gained popularity in the late nineteenth century.

As we study the first three chapters, we shall keep before us the divine purpose of this book: it is not to cause arguments and confusion but to encourage God's people in their walk with God, particularly when times are hard. In Christ's letters to the seven churches of Asia we have, revealed, His will for His people at all times and in all places. The Church in every age has needed to heed the Master's call; that is no less true today than it was when Jesus first spoke these words. So let us put aside our Western obsession with linear time and our speculations about where we might be on the divine calendar and instead open our ears to hear what the Spirit says to the churches.

What the Spirit reveals is Jesus Himself. This book is from Jesus and it is about Jesus. Like John, we will fall at His feet in worship and thanksgiving. Hearing His voice, we will turn and see Him in His risen and exalted glory. Our hearts will be strengthened as we discover afresh that He is the King of kings and Lord of lords and that all earth's proud empires will bow before Him. Just as importantly, we will wish to take on board His corrective words to His people. To have ears to hear is to have hearts that obey. We will not be judged by the accuracy of our speculations but by the faith obedience of our lives to the call of God.

Nor is this simply personal; the letters are addressed to churches and to their leaderships. Congregations have no automatic right to exist. Jesus moves among the candlesticks and He has the power to remove those that no longer fulfil their light-bearing ministry. His words are sobering, calling us as churches to consider our ways, to repent where needed, and to draw fresh grace from the One who 'is, and who was, and who is to come'. We dare not be complacent; the day of visitation is near and every church that bears the name of Christ will be examined by the One who stands among them, holding their messenger lights in His right hand.

The book was penned by John the apostle around the year AD 96 at a time when the Early Church was facing growing opposition under the reign of the Emperor Domitian. John, an elder in the Ephesian church, was a co-sufferer with his readers, having been banished to the island of Patmos as a prisoner of conscience for his proclamation of Christ's gospel.

He was 'in the Spirit' on the first day of the week, called the Lord's Day by the Early Church in honour of Christ's resurrection and as a reminder that He, and no other, is Lord. In this state of altered consciousness, John heard a loud voice instructing him to write a scroll to a circuit of seven churches: Ephesus, Smyrna, Pergamum, Thyatira, Sardis, Philadelphia and Laodicea. These churches were located in the Roman province of Asia which comprised the western seaboard of modern Turkey.

Angels play an important role in this book and John is sent one to assist him in his task, but it is not the angel that preoccupies him. Grace and peace come from the eternal Father, and from the sevenfold Holy Spirit – and from Jesus, 'the faithful witness, the firstborn from the dead, and the ruler of the kings of the earth'. It is Jesus whom John sees when he turns at the sound of the voice.

And what a sight! John had been the closest friend of Jesus on earth and had known Him in the reality of His humanity. True, he had seen the 'glory of the One and Only, who came from the Father' (John 1:14), but this is in a different league altogether. John sees a human form, but of such transcendent glory that it almost defies description. Every aspect is laden with biblical truth, from the priestly robe to the blazing eyes, from the golden sash to the burnished feet, from the thunderous voice to the two-edged sword, from the hoary head to the radiant sun. This is Christ, the Lord of glory, the First and the Last, the Living One, who was dead but now lives for ever and who holds the keys of death and Hades. Little wonder John is so overcome that he falls into a dead faint!

This is also the One who loves us and who has liberated us from the guilt, penalty and power of sin through the shedding of His own precious blood. He is the Lord who calls us to be His own people and to offer priestly service through Him. And He is coming back! There is no hint of a 'secret snatch' here. The Lord will be seen by everyone, even those who crucified Him. All saints and sinners, all angels and demons, will behold the King in His glory – and worship!

WEEK 1

Ephesus – The Call to Love

Opening Icebreaker

Darken the room and then light seven candles. Give one to each member of the group along with a label of one of the seven churches – Ephesus, Smyrna, Pergamum, Thyatira, Sardis, Philadelphia, Laodicea. Ask the candleholders to imagine they are the guardians of their flame. How would they feel if their flame were blown out? Blow each flame out in turn and note how dark the world has become!

Bible Readings

- Revelation 1:1–19
- Revelation 2:1–7
- 1 Corinthians 13:1–13

Key Verse: 'Yet I hold this against you: You have forsaken your first love.' (2:4)

Focus: Service, faithfulness and truth must all be motivated by love.

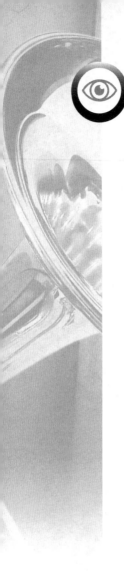

Opening Our Eyes

The Ephesian church was founded around AD 55 by the apostle Paul during his third missionary journey. From its origins, the church was noted for its sound doctrine, charismatic power, evangelistic zeal and passionate devotion to the Lord. Many converts came from pagan backgrounds and publicly burned their occult books and artefacts.

Ephesus was a metropolitan seaport of around 250,000 people, situated on the Cayster River and on the main trading route from Rome to the Orient. Capital of the Roman province and a deeply pagan city, it was home to one of the seven wonders of the world – the great temple of Artemis. So great was the early impact of the gospel that it affected the trade in silver tourist trinkets and provoked a riot. Nevertheless, the gospel flourished and spread throughout the province, bringing to birth churches in at least six other cities.

Now, some forty years later, Jesus conducts a review of these churches and, through John, publishes His findings in a circular to be read out to all the churches. This gives us a clue to the identity of the 'angels' of the churches: the seven stars. These are not heavenly beings, since Jesus would hardly write to an angel via the apostle John. The word means 'messenger' and the most likely person would be a member of the eldership with a preaching and public reading ministry. In an age of low literacy and few writings this was an important role requiring a person who was literate, articulate and trustworthy (1 Tim. 4:13–15).

Jesus commences by commending the Ephesian church for its hard work. These highly motivated activists served the church and the surrounding community with zeal. They were tenacious, too. The riot in Paul's day reminds us that this city of idols did not take kindly to those who worshipped Jesus – nor did the large Jewish colony in the city. Social ostracism and trade boycotts against followers of the Way made life difficult, and John himself was exiled for the sake of the gospel. Yet these believers remained undaunted by adversity.

Having benefited from the illustrious ministries of Paul, Priscilla and Aquila, Apollos, Timothy and John, the Ephesian church was committed to sound doctrine. Paul had warned that savage wolves would come, false apostles whose perverse doctrines would devastate the flock of God (Acts 20:28–31). They arrived in the shape of the Nicolaitans. The word means 'people destroyer' and may be symbolic. Having given a fair hearing to these 'apostles' the Ephesians had rightly judged their compromised teaching and behaviour to be false.

There was a problem, however; for all their evangelical zeal, determination and orthodoxy they had lost their first love. The bride was no longer intoxicated with the Bridegroom. The church had fallen from the heights of its pristine love for Jesus. For all its fine virtues, the light of passion had faded. Christ calls them to remembrance and to repentance. It is as much a sin to serve the Lord without loving Him, as it is a nonsense to love the Lord without serving Him.

So serious is it that Jesus warns He could remove the church's candlestick. If you have ears to hear then take note. Those who do – the overcomers – will inherit their Eden; they will eat of the tree of eternal life that had been barred to Adam and Eve. Those who truly love the Lord will enjoy His love for ever.

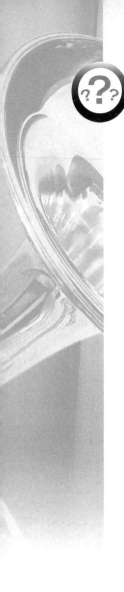

Discussion Starters

1. How do we practically repent of having lost our first love for the Lord?

2. We love Him because He first loved us. How did Jesus show His love for us (see Rev. 1:5)?

3. If Jesus threatened to remove a lampstand, how would we know when it had happened and what could we do to prevent it?

4. How can we ensure that every activity of our lives and churches is characterised by fervent love for the Lord?

5. In what ways do you think doctrinal error destroys people?

_____

_____

_____

_____

_____

6. What are the means that we should use to test the truth of a teaching or a teacher?

_____

_____

_____

_____

_____

7. What do you think paradise will be like?

_____

_____

_____

_____

_____

Personal Application

Are you zealous for the truth? Is your diary filled with meetings? Are you determined to keep going whatever the circumstances? That makes you an admirable Stoic; it does not make you a Christian (Matt. 7:21–23). Love without service is false, but service without love is merely cold duty (1 Cor. 13:1–3). A true believer is someone who loves the Lord with passionate devotion and it is that which inspires their love for others (1 John 3:16; 4:19). Do you need to recover your first love for Him? If so, you will find Him more than willing to respond to your prayers.

Seeing Jesus in the Scriptures

Jesus holds the seven stars and walks in the midst of the seven churches (Rev. 1:12–13, 16). He is always closer than we think! He observes not only our every meeting, but the lives of each member. This is a tremendous encouragement, but also a challenge, for if Jesus were to write an OFSTED report on your church, or your life, how would it fare? Would it be a record of love for Him and for others? Would it note that fervent love motivated all the activities and witness of God's people? This is the light that Jesus, the Light of the World, would have shine from His lampstands. We should take heed, for He has the right to remove the lampstands that no longer glow with His glory. The wise virgins in the parable ensured that they had enough oil to keep their lamps burning until the Master came. We should do likewise.

WEEK 2

Smyrna – The Call to Suffer

Opening Icebreaker

If you were taken to court charged with being a Christian, what evidence would be presented to find you guilty of the charge?

Bible Readings

- Revelation 1:1–19
- Revelation 2:8–11
- 1 Peter 4:12–19

Key Verse: 'Do not be afraid of what you are about to suffer.' (2:10)

Focus: Persecution is an unavoidable reality for true followers of Christ.

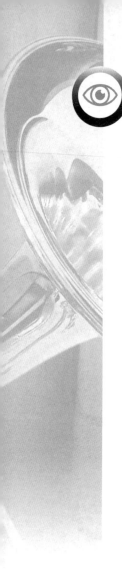

Opening Our Eyes

Smyrna was a prosperous maritime city that lay thirty-five miles to the north of Ephesus. It was famed for its municipal magnificence. A long-time ally of Rome, the city was a centre of emperor worship and possessed a prized temple dedicated to the Emperor Tiberius.

The church in Smyrna was undergoing persecution. In a city where acknowledging that 'Caesar is Lord' was a civic duty, a refusal to do so was tantamount to rebellion. To say instead 'Jesus is Lord' was, and is, a political statement.

The authorities were understandably suspicious of the church but the situation was greatly exacerbated by the slander of Jews fanatically opposed to the gospel. Being themselves legally exempt from sacrificial obligations to Caesar, they did not hesitate to incite rumour and hatred against those who claimed that Jesus was the Messiah. As a consequence, Christians had been impoverished and blasphemed, and worse was to come. Jesus prophesies a short but intense period of persecution that will include imprisonment and even death for the faithful. Indeed, the unholy alliance of the Jewish fundamentalists and the Roman Empire against the church continued well into the next century. When the saintly Polycarp, bishop of Smyrna, was martyred on 22 February AD 156, the Jews were the most zealous to call for his death, and to fetch the wood for the fire.

Jesus has not abandoned His Church. Far from it.
He knows of the slander against His people and His assessment of the situation is clear. In words reminiscent of John 8:44 ('You belong to your father, the devil'), He describes these Jews as 'a synagogue of Satan' – perhaps a term they had slanderously used against the church.

Smyrna – The Call to Suffer

Jewish opposition was nothing new. Paul had been dogged by the same fanaticism. Having himself once been a persecutor of the Church, he does not mince his words concerning the perversity of his opponents (1 Thess. 2:14–16). He reminds us, too, that salvation is by grace, not by race. The only true Jews are those whose hearts are circumcised (Rom. 2:28–29; Gal. 6:15–16).

In spite of their adversity, Jesus tells the Smyrnian believers that they are truly rich. They may have been impoverished by their adversaries but there is much more to life than material prosperity. After all, what is the use of someone gaining the whole world at the expense of their own soul? The believers may look like losers in the eyes of people, but they are the winners in the eyes of God, and He will honour them with the victor's crown of life.

This surely is the point: believers engaged in spiritual warfare should not fear those whose limit is to kill the body. God exercises a power beyond the grave (Luke 12:4–5). Fear Him! There is a prospect of death beyond death (Rev. 20:11–15; 21:8). Those who stand firm in the face of persecution will be entirely spared the horror of the second death. However, Satan himself, who in times of persecution 'prowls around like a roaring lion looking for someone to devour' (1 Pet. 5:8), will have no escape. The devil, who instigated the imprisonment of the saints, will be cast into that eternal prison, the lake of fire. As for those whom he has tormented, it will turn out to be no more than a permitted testing to prove the true worth of God's children – and they will come forth victorious.

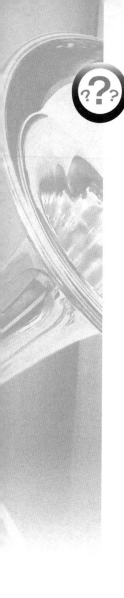

Discussion Starters

1. Why do you think people persecute Christians?

2. We are all engaged in spiritual warfare. What does this mean in your daily life and in the life of your church?

3. Sometimes the Church has been guilty of anti-Semitism. How can we give due recognition to the historic opposition of the Jews to the gospel and yet avoid the evils of anti-Semitism?

4. In an age of consumerism, what constitutes true riches?

5. What effect should the resurrection of Christ have on us when we are facing opposition for our faith?

_____

_____

_____

_____

_____

6. What does it mean when Jesus says He holds the keys of death and Hades?

_____

_____

_____

_____

7. How do you talk about the second death to your family and friends, your colleagues and neighbours?

_____

_____

_____

_____

Personal Application

Jesus and the apostles were realistic about the cost of being a disciple. All who truly follow Christ will experience persecution to a greater or lesser degree (2 Tim. 3:12; Phil. 1:29; 1 Pet. 4:12–19). They hated Jesus; they will hate us (John 15:18). This is part of what it means to bear the offence of the cross. It is also a matter of spiritual warfare. To follow Jesus is not only to challenge the ways of the world; it is to mount an assault on the kingdom of darkness.

Jesus encourages us not to be afraid in times of persecution. Like the apostles, we may rejoice that we are counted worthy to suffer for Christ. Paul, himself no stranger to persecution, reminds us that those who suffer with Him will also reign with Him in glory (Rom. 8:17).

Seeing Jesus in the Scriptures

Jesus is the First and the Last; He is the eternal Son of God. He is also the Man who died and was raised from the dead. Having been the faithful witness who embodied and proclaimed the Father's will, He has become the fountainhead of a new creation. Yet this is not an otherworldly kingdom. Jesus is King of kings and Lord of lords. He reigns over Caesar and every other world leader. Satan no longer has that right. It is Jesus who now holds the keys of death and Hades. The only prospect for Satan is the second death, along with all who chose to serve him. However, those who acknowledge that Jesus is Lord will enjoy everlasting life.

WEEK 3

Pergamum –
The Call to Truth

Opening Icebreaker

Based on the scripture, 'I have hidden your word in my heart that I might not sin against you' (Psa. 119:11), name a truth or a scripture that you have purposefully written on your heart to keep you from a particular sin.

Bible Readings

- Revelation 1:1–19
- Revelation 2:12–17
- John 17:13–19
- 2 Timothy 3:12–4:5

Key Verse: 'Yet you remain true to my name. You did not renounce your faith in me ...' (2:13)

Focus: The truth of the Scriptures is the foundation for holy living.

Opening Our Eyes

North of Smyrna and fifteen miles inland lay the dark city of Pergamum. Overshadowed by an acropolis on a 330-metre-high hill, and with a great altar dedicated to Zeus, Pergamum was a centre where paganism and politics went hand in hand. Jesus described it as the place where Satan's throne is.

The church had been through tough times; one of their members, Antipas, had been executed for testifying to the truth about Jesus. This might have cowed the other believers, but instead they had remained impressively faithful to their Lord. However, there was a problem.

Some of the believers were falling for an ancient and destructive compromise. It went like this: confess that Jesus is Lord and maintain a spiritual life, but have a secular life, too – a kind of 'Saturday night clubbing, Sunday morning church' lifestyle.

In Moses' time, Balaam had been commissioned to curse the Israelites. Prevented by God, he appears to have proposed that his financier, King Balak, lure them instead into the Moabite world of pagan partying and promiscuously available women (Num. 25:1–3). The ploy proved very successful and it provoked an epidemic that killed 24,000 of God's people. If war against God's people couldn't destroy them, then seduction might.

In Pergamum, the instruments of Balaam's deceit were the Nicolaitans. Their false teaching encouraged believers to compromise their behaviour, to 'mix it'. False doctrine sooner or later leads to false living (2 Pet. 2:1–2). Jude explains that such people pervert the grace of God into a licence to sin. They do so by arguing that freedom in Christ allows you to embrace the immorality of the world around and yet still be saved (Jude 3–4). 'Salvation is not by works, so behaviour doesn't count. It's only what you believe that matters,' runs their perverse argument. This is heresy – a false doctrine called antinomianism – and Jesus warns the Pergamum church that they will have Him to contend with if they don't deal with it. It won't be 'gentle Jesus, meek and mild', either. He will fight against the heretics with the lethal power of His Word.

Arrogant worldliness justified by fine-sounding but false teaching can be powerfully attractive. Who would not wish to be part of a liberal, exciting, sophisticated group with its 'freedom', rather than be lumped with the killjoy 'legalists'? Those who refused to compromise may well have felt they were missing out; but for those who made the right choice, Jesus offered something considerably better than idolatrous party food and a dose of casual sex. The lives of the faithful will be truly fulfilled; their inner hunger will be met with the sacred manna that was hidden in the golden jar in the ark of the covenant (Heb. 9:4). They will feed on the Living Bread Himself (John 6:31–35,48–51). Partaking of this food will nourish you for ever … and with no hangover.

They will also be given an engraved white stone. Opinions vary as to the nature of this stone but it is most likely the equivalent of an individually coded security pass guaranteeing us access to the greatest party of all – the marriage supper of the Lamb. Much better than a ticket to Vanity Fair! The new name represents our new identity in Christ and, although we share that identity with all God's people, it is also unique and precious to each one of us.

Discussion Starters

1. Why do you think doctrine matters in an age of so-called tolerance (see John 17:13–19)?

2. What is unique and non-negotiable about Jesus?

3. Where do you especially see satanic deception at work in our contemporary world?

4. How can we best communicate the truth of the gospel in a pluralistic age?

5. What does it mean to take 'the sword of the Spirit, which is the word of God' (Eph. 6:17)?

_____

_____

_____

_____

_____

6. How do we feed on the Living Bread in our daily lives?

_____

_____

_____

_____

_____

7. How would you describe the new name that Jesus gives to those who overcome?

_____

_____

_____

_____

_____

Personal Application

Truth matters. Jesus said, 'you will know the truth, and the truth will set you free' (John 8:32). It is not freedom to do as we please. Bodies that were once slaves of sin now need to become slaves of righteousness (Rom. 6:13–14). Holiness is more than religious belief and Sunday piety; it reveals itself in an ethical lifestyle. Love is more than a sentimental feeling; it encapsulates heart obedience to the commandments (Rom. 13:8–10). The test of the rightness of any doctrine is whether or not it produces gospel righteousness in our lives.

We must study the Word and give ourselves to sound teaching, but every word needs to be applied consistently to our daily behaviour (2 Tim. 3:16–17). How well do we know *and display* the true doctrine of Christ?

Seeing Jesus in the Scriptures

Jesus is the truth, and the two-edged sword of the Word of God proceeds from His mouth. The words He speaks are Spirit and life. This is the same sword of the Spirit that we must wield in spiritual warfare. It alone has the penetrating power to expose the reality of people's hearts (Eph. 6:17; Heb. 4:12).

Christ's voice is also like 'the sound of rushing waters'. Think of a thundering mighty waterfall. The word of the Lord is no plaintive, faint whimper. When it comes it is overwhelming, drowning out all others with its majestic power. Take heed! The Father says, 'This is my Son, whom I love. Listen to him!' (Mark 9:7).

WEEK 4

Thyatira –
The Call to Holiness

Opening Icebreaker

Ask each member of the group to name a cultural idol that they have had to forsake in order to follow Jesus.

Bible Readings

- Revelation 1:1–19
- Revelation 2:18–29
- Acts 15:22–29
- 1 Corinthians 10:6–10,21–22; 11:28–30

Key Verse: 'Nevertheless, I have this against you: You tolerate that woman Jezebel, who calls herself a prophetess. By her teaching she misleads my servants into sexual immorality and the eating of food sacrificed to idols.' (2:20)

Focus: We are called to refuse the sophisticated seductions of immorality and idolatry.

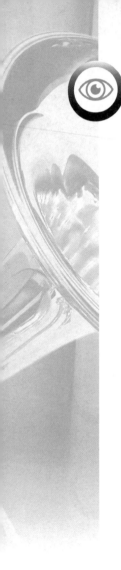

Opening Our Eyes

South-east of Pergamum lay the commercial and industrial city of Thyatira. The business woman, Lydia, a founding convert of the Philippian church, had originated from here – Acts 16:14. The church in Thyatira had done well and Jesus commends it for its growth in love, faith, service, and tenacity. For all that, it was a church in crisis.

A prophetess, codenamed Jezebel, had gained significant influence in the church. Her teaching was, like that of the Nicolaitans, beguiling God's people into idolatry and immorality. The difference here is that she held a position of major influence in the church, possibly as a leader's wife, and her teaching had seduced a large number of believers.

The codename recalls Jezebel, the notorious wife of King Ahab, ruler of Israel from 874–853 BC. Her father was a priest of Astarte, and Jezebel had imported the Baal fertility cult from her home town of Sidon. Hounding the Lord's prophets to death, she established a temple in Samaria with 850 cult priests (1 Kings 16:30–32). Earth magic and sexual immorality became rife.

The Jezebel of Thyatira had launched a 'deeper spirituality' society within the church while continuing attendance at the normal meetings. Her esoteric teaching was bewitching and a significant number had been initiated into her occult mysteries. However, the inner sanctum for the initiates was not a holy of holies. It was her own bedroom. Here, far from celebrating the body and blood of Jesus with bread and wine, they would partake instead of a perverse communion of blood-soaked idol meat and sex.

Jesus sees through closed doors and false spirituality. He searches hearts and minds with a fiery gaze. The so-called 'deep secrets' of this woman are the deep secrets of Satan! Her heart is arrogant. In spite of having been granted time to repent she has refused to change. Consequently, her bed of adultery will become a bed of sickness and that will be the fate of all who share in her sins. Likewise, the children born of her adulteries will die. It's stern stuff but Jesus will not permit His church to degenerate into just another pagan fertility cult. The church leaders should have dealt with this woman. History teaches us that judgment follows whenever God's people fall into such unholy behaviour. Remember Aaron's golden calf, Elijah's drought, the Assyrian invasion, the Babylonian captivity? Learn the lesson, lest you fall, Paul cautions the Corinthians (1 Cor. 10:6–10,21–22; 11:28–30).

Not all had been mesmerised by this woman's perverse charms and Jesus brings them words of encouragement. They do not need to punish themselves or react into extreme self-denial (Matt. 11:30). The only requirement is to keep faithful and avoid idolatrous meat and sexual immorality (Acts 15:28–29).

Knowledge is power, but the meek will inherit the earth. Jesus promises the faithful that they will share in His rule over the nations (Psa. 2:8–9). Given the arrogance and rebellion of the nations, He will rule 'with an iron sceptre', for they must respect the Holy One of Israel.

He will also give His faithful followers the morning star. This is the planet Venus, so often connected with immorality in the pagan mind. Jesus claims the morning star as His own Messianic title in Revelation 22:16. He is the light in the darkness and the hope for a new day that challenges us to live worthy of the light (Rom. 13:11–14).

Discussion Starters

1. What thoughts and impressions does the idea of holiness conjure up in your mind?

2. What is your response to the fact that Jesus knows everything about us all of the time?

3. Why do you think Jesus (and ourselves) will need an 'iron sceptre' to rule over the nations?

4. Where and how do you think the Jezebel spirit might manifest itself today?

5. How would you answer those who say that Internet porn is harmless for Christians because it does not involve an actual sexual encounter?

6. To what extent do you think there is a connection between a lack of holiness and sickness?

7. 'The heavens declare the glory of God' (Psa. 19:1). The morning star is the planet Venus and should remind us of Jesus. How can we use this fact to counter the occult superstition associated with horoscopes and point to a better way?

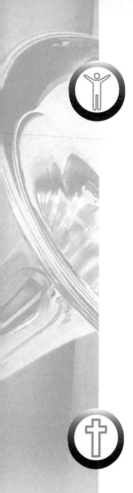

Personal Application

There are three temptations: the lust of the flesh, the lust of the eyes, and the pride of life; three sources of temptation: the world, the flesh, the devil; and there are three satanic weapons: persecution, deception and seduction.

All these can be overcome by the blood of the Lamb and the word of our testimony. The One within us is greater than the devil. The Holy Spirit guides us into all truth. God's Word countermands the devil's lies. Our faith grants us victory over the world. God has given us great and precious promises to enable us escape the corruption of the world.

Jesus wants us to win! Check out that your life is committed to a genuine holiness based on truth and love and a vision of Him.

Seeing Jesus in the Scriptures

John sees Jesus clothed in priestly glory. It is reminiscent of the Transfiguration. As Peter puts it, 'we were eye-witnesses of his majesty' (2 Pet. 1:16). In the letter to Thyatira it is the blazing eyes and fiery feet that capture our attention. They speak of holiness and zeal. Jesus knows everything! There is no hiding from the Holy One of Israel before whom the hearts of all are laid bare (Jer. 17:10). Nor is He indifferent. His feet burn with the passion of the gospel for they are the feet that were pierced for our sins. Surely we need to recapture that holy fire in our own lives and churches. Love righteousness; hate iniquity! Be holy, for the Lord your God is holy.

WEEK 5

Sardis – The Call to Life

Opening Icebreaker

Share personal stories of your first real encounter with the Holy Spirit and a recent experience of the Spirit in your life.

Bible Readings

- Revelation 1:1–19
- Revelation 3:1–6
- Isaiah 29:9–14

Key Verse: 'To the angel of the church in Sardis write: These are the words of him who holds the seven spirits of God and the seven stars. I know your deeds; you have a reputation of being alive, but you are dead.' (3:1)

Focus: Spiritual life will depart from a church that bases its reputation on past glories.

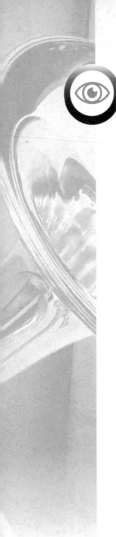

Opening Our Eyes

Sardis, the former wealthy capital of Lydia, lay fifty miles inland of Smyrna above the Hermus river valley. Once an impregnable fortress city, it had grown complacent and, through lack of vigilance, had fallen to the Persians, and later to the Greeks, before Rome took control.

The church, like the city, was living on its past glories. It had a name, a pedigree, an active programme – all the machinery of a reputable, well-established church. But it was dead. Or as near as makes no difference. It had lost the vibrant power of the Holy Spirit and descended into complacent nominalism; it had a name but no spiritual reality. This church could operate on manpower alone; it no longer needed the living presence of Christ and hadn't even noticed that He was absent.

The church in Sardis hadn't been persecuted; its doctrine was sound; there is no hint of public sin. It had simply died on the inside. People were baptised but not spiritually reborn; they took communion but did not feed on the Bread of Life. They attended the services and had fellowship with each other but their hearts were distant from God (Isa. 29:13).

God is unimpressed by this form of outward piety (2 Tim. 3:5). It doesn't come up to His requirements. He wants much more than 'all present and correct' in an ecclesiastical morgue. Jesus urges the remaining few faithful ones not to succumb to the fumes of spiritual death that waft through the church. They must remember how the gospel had come to them, as it had to the Corinthians and others, 'not with wise and persuasive words, but with a demonstration of the Spirit's power' (1 Cor. 2:4). For this church had been one of those founded out of the mighty move of God emanating from Ephesus during Paul's ministry. They must wake up and

repent before it is too late. If not, they will have a divine
visitation of the kind best avoided. As a thief comes
without warning to steal while people sleep, so Jesus will
unexpectedly strip the church of its remaining assets. And
why not, if it is dead? It was a pertinent warning, given
the city's history of sudden invasion.

Nominal Christianity is usually a cloak for sin; behind
the outwardly correct person lies the licentious person.
Jesus' penetrating gaze which exposed the hypocrisy
of the Pharisees (Matt. 23:27–28), likewise saw through
the formalism of the church in Sardis. However, a few
had kept themselves clean in spite of the prevailing
worldliness. Jesus promises them the honour of walking
in His presence wearing unsoiled white robes. This is
more than a mere symbol of holiness. Eternal life itself
is at stake. These people are in the Lamb's book of life
and, when the roll is called, Jesus will acknowledge their
names before the Father, the Judge of all the earth.

The sober truth is that you can be on the church
members' roll but not in the Lamb's book of life, and the
consequences of that are dire. How awful to be a nominal
member without real spiritual life and to finish up in the
lake of fire when you might instead have been a resident
in paradise city (Rev. 20:15; 21:27). What a contrast to
those who overcome this deadly sleeping sickness. They
will never be blotted out from the Lamb's book of life,
and that is guaranteed by Jesus Himself.

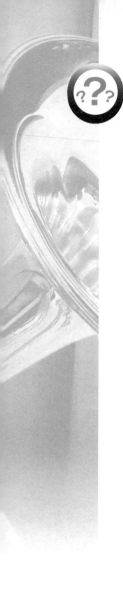

Discussion Starters

1. What do you think are the marks of a church of repute that lacks real spiritual life?

2. The world is full of temptations to 'soil our clothes'. Name those you consider the most prevalent in the nominal Church.

3. How can we be sure that our names are in the Lamb's book of life and not just on the church membership roll?

4. A formal acknowledgement that all believers receive the Holy Spirit is not enough. How does that become a reality in our lives?

5. Why do you think the Holy Spirit is described as the 'seven spirits'? What does this mean in our lives?

_____

_____

_____

_____

6. What message would you give to someone whom you knew to be a church attendee but who did not appear to know the Lord in a personal way?

_____

_____

_____

_____

7. How can we sustain the spiritual life of our church and avoid slipping into spiritual death?

_____

_____

_____

_____

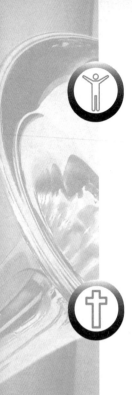

Personal Application

You may have been a church member for a long time, but are you really spiritually alive? Have you been born again? Have you truly and consciously received the Holy Spirit, so that your life is constantly transformed and energised by His presence and power? Do you know that your name is written in the Lamb's book of life? If the answer is yes, then you may be assured of your salvation. If it is no, then you should earnestly seek the Lord, perhaps with the help of others, until you are sure.

Seeing Jesus in the Scriptures

Jesus holds the seven spirits of God and the seven stars. The seven spirits of God are also the seven lamps that blaze before God's throne (Rev. 4:5) and they are the seven eyes of the Lamb of God (Rev. 5:6; see Zech. 4:2, 10). The symbolism reminds us that the Holy Spirit is the Spirit of Christ who is within the Church, before the throne, and sent into all the world. The number seven speaks of the diversity and the perfection of His work. The eye being the lamp that lights our inner self (Matt. 6:22–23), so Christ, beholding the throne, is filled with the light of life.

The seven stars represent the seven messengers of the churches. Their proclamation – representing the testimony of the whole Church – must be delivered under the anointing of the Holy Spirit, for this is Christ's message. 'The Spirit gives life; the flesh counts for nothing. The words I have spoken to you are spirit and they are life' (John 6:63).

WEEK 6

Philadelphia – The Call to Enter

Opening Icebreaker

Ask members of your group to show some proof of identity and to explain why they carry it.

Bible Readings

* Revelation 1:1–19
* Revelation 3:7–13
* Ephesians 2:11–22
* 1 Peter 2:4–10
* Acts 2:25–32

Key Verse: 'I know your deeds. See, I have placed before you an open door that no-one can shut. I know that you have little strength, yet you have kept my word and have not denied my name.' (3:8)

Focus: The true people of God are those who confess that Jesus is the Messiah.

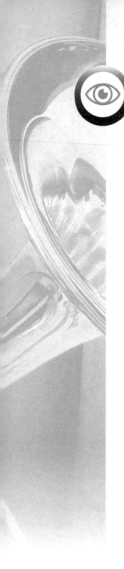

Opening Our Eyes

Philadelphia was a prosperous city situated twenty-eight miles south-east of Sardis at the junction of several major trade routes. The Philadelphian church was not strong, but it was faithful in spite of evident opposition from the local Jewish synagogue.

The issue Jesus addresses concerns the identity of the true people of God. To whom belongs the kingdom of God? To the Jews, who had rejected Jesus of Nazareth as their Messiah, or to that company of Jews and Gentiles who found themselves united in the New Man, Jesus, to form the new Israel (Eph. 2:14–16,19)?

There can be no doubt; Jesus is the true Messiah. He holds the key of David and entrance into the Messianic kingdom is determined by Him and no other. He has opened the door to all who confess Him 'the Christ, the Son of the living God' (Matt. 16:16), and that includes these Philadelphian believers. However much the unbelieving Jews tried to exclude them, Jesus has wedged the door firmly open. The kingdom is for people of every nation, tribe and tongue – whoever calls on the name of the Lord will be saved. This open door is at the heart of the new covenant missionary mandate (Matt. 28:18–20). Jews with their advantages, Gentiles far away, they can all find salvation the same way: by grace through faith in Jesus Christ our Lord.

The Church, consisting of all those who confess Jesus as Lord and Christ, is a spiritual house (1 Pet. 2:4–6). The believers who hold fast their confession of His Messiahship will be pillars in the temple, a position of security that they will never forfeit. They are citizens of heaven, God's own people (1 Pet. 2:9–10). His name is on their identity documents; so is their homeland – the new Jerusalem descending from heaven – and it is endorsed by Jesus' own signature.

What, then, of those Jews who sought to deny the church this privilege? As with those at Ephesus, Jesus describes them as liars and 'a synagogue of Satan'. They who should have received Him as their Messiah had sold out to the devil. Jesus made it clear that a tree is known by its fruit, whatever its label: 'Therefore I tell you that the kingdom of God will be taken away from you and given to a people who will produce its fruit' (Matt. 21:43).

All is not lost, however. Jesus the Messiah prophesies that they will come to acknowledge His loving favour on His Church. This was Paul's desire and hope for his people (Rom. 11:13–15,25–27). It is an eschatological hope, for Jesus is coming back. Yet His return will be preceded by a period of great trial that will affect all humankind. The nature of these trials is unpacked throughout the seven parallel cycles of the book of Revelation, until they culminate in the return of Christ.

The Church will not be spared this time of testing, but it will be kept safe by Jesus. This view is confirmed by Revelation 7:14 and many other scriptures. The key lies in Jesus' high priestly prayer: 'My prayer is not that you take them out of the world but that you protect them from the evil one' (John 17:15). The testing will prove the integrity and tenacity of God's people, while the world's sin, rebellion, corruption and deceit will be exposed for all to see.

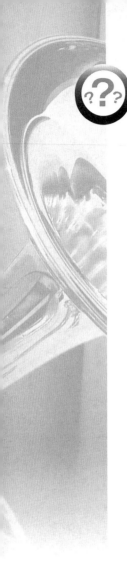

Discussion Starters

1. What do you understand by the phrase, 'the kingdom of God'?

2. What would you say to someone who enquired about becoming one of God's people?

3. What does it mean to you that Jesus holds the key of David?

4. How would you communicate to a Jew that Jesus is the Christ, the Son of the living God?

5. How would you describe the fruit that denotes the true members of Christ's kingdom?

_____

_____

_____

_____

_____

6. Why do you think God will let times of trial come upon the whole world?

_____

_____

_____

_____

_____

7. What does it mean to be protected from the evil one when undergoing times of testing?

_____

_____

_____

_____

_____

Personal Application

If you have confessed that Jesus is the Christ and received Him into your life, you are a member of the spiritual house, a living stone, being built into a holy temple to the Lord. Your citizenship is in heaven. One day you will find yourself at home, by divine right, in the new Jerusalem. When Jesus returns you will be part of that great company who have come through the trials to welcome the Saviour.

People may laugh, tell you you've got it all wrong, despise your church. Be faithful to your good confession, for something wonderful awaits you. As Paul puts it: 'Now there is in store for me the crown of righteousness, which the Lord, the righteous Judge, will award to me on that day – and not only to me, but also to all who have longed for his appearing' (2 Tim. 4:8).

Seeing Jesus in the Scriptures

Jesus holds all the keys. Keys represent authority, and Jesus has authority over death and Hades. He also holds the key of David. He is the legitimate descendant of King David, as both His genealogies testify (Matt. 1:1,6; Luke 3:23,31). He is the One of whom David prophesied (Psa. 110:1–7) and He is 'the Lion of the tribe of Judah, the Root of David' (Rev. 5:5).

Peter takes this theme up on the Day of Pentecost, declaring that although David was dead, he prophesied the resurrection of one of his descendants, namely, the Christ (Acts 2:25–32). Jesus of Nazareth is risen, so He is that Man. Hallelujah!

WEEK 7

Laodicea –
The Call to Authenticity

Opening Icebreaker

Serve the members of your group with lukewarm (30–35°C, 87–93°F) tea or coffee. Observe their reactions and then ask them what they thought of the drink.

Bible Readings

- Revelation 1:1–19
- Revelation 3:14–22
- Isaiah 55:1–13

Key Verse: 'So, because you are lukewarm – neither hot nor cold – I am about to spit you out of my mouth.' (3:16)

Focus: We should live up to the claims that we make as God's people.

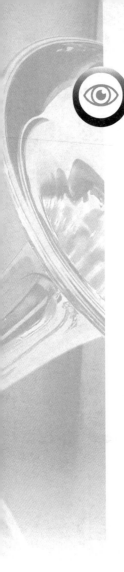

Opening Our Eyes

The last of the churches to receive this circular letter was located in Laodicea. An exceptionally prosperous city 160 km due east inland of Ephesus, Laodicea was a strategically placed centre of banking, medicine and manufacturing and the church had benefited from its material prosperity. Paul knew of Laodicea and instructed that his Colossian letter be read to the Laodiceans also (Col. 4:16).

There was no heresy in this church, no persecution, no immorality. It was simply lukewarm. Jesus put this down to their arrogant self-sufficiency. The church had need of nothing. Prosperous, fashionable, urbane, with access to private healthcare and major road systems, these people didn't even notice that Jesus was missing.

These complacent Christians were living under a terrible delusion, reminiscent of the tale of the emperor's new clothes. Believing themselves to be something, they were actually nothing. These privileged and sophisticated city people were, in the eyes of Jesus, more like desperate refugees. For all their imagined finery they were 'wretched, pitiful, poor, blind and naked'. Their shopping sprees had actually impoverished them, for they had shopped in the wrong places and for the wrong things. As if consumer comforts could ever produce spiritual life!

Jesus was sickened by this church, so much so that He was about to spit it out. The reason was simple: it didn't deliver what it promised when He tested the water. Jesus liked hot water; He liked cold water; but this lukewarm stuff was disgusting! His language is understood by reference to Laodicea's water supply. The city depended on two aqueducts; one from Colossae that supplied cold drinkable water, and one from the medicinal hot springs near Hierapolis that were great for aches and pains. This

Laodicea – The Call to Authenticity

WEEK SEVEN

latter supply was not only merely lukewarm by the time it reached Laodicea, but the concentrated mineral content made it virtually undrinkable. The church was fit for neither one thing nor the other; spiritually speaking, it could neither refresh with cool water nor heal with a hot spa. Yet it should have been able to do both. After all, it was the church of Jesus Christ!

Yet the Lord loves His Church. His stern words are those of a father, not a judge. He calls for zealous repentance and urges His people to change their shopping habits and buy from Him. Jesus even offers a home delivery service. He is on the doorstep, knocking for admission. Those who open the door will have the privilege of entertaining the most important guest of all, and of sampling His wares. In words reminiscent of Isaiah 55:1, He has on offer the refined gold of true, spiritual, prosperity; He has the white robes of His righteousness to cover the embarrassing nakedness of their self-righteousness; Laodicea produced a famed compound to treat eye diseases – Jesus can provide a cure for their spiritual blindness. As with those two disciples on the Emmaus Road (Luke 24:28–32), if they invite Jesus in He will open their eyes and set their hearts ablaze.

Overcoming sometimes means dealing with hard obstacles. Here it means overcoming the cloying consumerism of a comfortable society that saps and pollutes spiritual life to the point of uselessness. Worldly advancement does not compare to spiritual honour. Those who desire to be authentic are invited to sit with Jesus in the heavenly places, at the right hand of the Father. The voice of the Spirit is unmistakable. Do you have ears that can hear it?

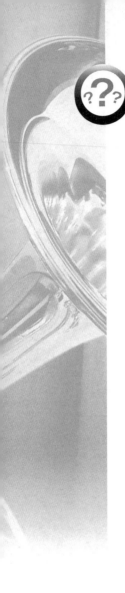

Discussion Starters

1. How would you apply the message of this letter to the consumerism of our day?

2. What do you understand by true prosperity?

3. In what ways do you think the Church is self-satisfied and complacent today? How would you address this?

4. Jesus opened the eyes of the blind. What is the nature of spiritual blindness and eye disease today?

5. Jesus' words are stern but loving. How do we respond to the 'kindness and sternness of God' (Rom. 11:22)?

_____

_____

_____

_____

_____

6. What does it mean to open the door to Jesus?

_____

_____

_____

_____

7. How would you demonstrate that your church was as authentic as Jesus?

_____

_____

_____

_____

_____

Personal Application

Is it authentic? I want the real thing. We expect things to do what they say they will do. Salt should be salty, says Jesus. If it isn't, we throw it away (Matt. 5:13). Drinking water should be fresh and clear; hot water should be hot. A church should deliver spiritual life. Grace should characterise every member, and love be manifest in their relationships. Worship should be fervent; prayer should be intimate. Teaching should be anointed truth addressing the realities of life. The presence of the Lord should be tangible. People should be refreshed and healed. The world should feel the touch of heaven from our daily presence and witness. If this is not so then something is wrong. It needs to be put right. We need to open the door to Jesus afresh and let Him come back in.

Seeing Jesus in the Scriptures

Jesus is the Affirmative, the great Yes Indeed! He never lies and never deceives. There is no unreality about His claims. He is the Authentic One, the faithful and true witness. All the promises of God find their fulfilment in Him (2 Cor. 1:20). Whatever other religions and gurus may offer, Jesus is the only way to the Father (John 14:6) and He is the one mediator between God and humanity (1 Tim. 2:5).

As such, He is also the Lord of all creation and the firstborn from the dead. He is the authentic Source, the Fountainhead, and the rightful ruler of all rulers and authorities. 'To him be … glory and power, for ever and ever!' Amen.

Leader's Notes

Reading the book of Revelation, you may feel daunted by the complex imagery. Don't worry; although a full understanding requires an intimate knowledge of the whole Bible, most readers can grasp the main themes without difficulty. The book only becomes complicated when we impose schemes of interpretation that seek to fit it exclusively to a particular time or place in world history. This is unwarranted, unnecessary, and serves only to distract from its real thrust.

With this in mind, steer your group away from speculation and focus instead on edification. What does this have to teach us about our lives and churches today? The book is a revelation of Jesus Christ, so our aim is to worship Him. He speaks words to the seven churches that are relevant for our churches today. What do we need to hear? How should we change our behaviour in the light of His words? What comfort can we draw from them?

Read the Introduction to tune your group into these studies before going on to the first session. Revelation 1 is read each week to keep us focused on the vision of Jesus. As you work through the sessions delegate the different sections to others.

Week 1: Ephesus – The Call to Love

Icebreaker

The opening icebreaker is intended to set the scene and familiarise your group with the seven churches. It is likely that John saw his vision during the night hours, otherwise the impact of the lampstands, the stars and the vision of Jesus would be lost in the Aegean sunshine. Explain that each church was an oil lamp and each star a messenger.

Aim of the Session

For background, read about the founding of the Ephesian church in Acts 19. The gospel affected the whole province, leading to the probable founding of the other churches.

This whole book is a message from Jesus. The messengers are those who pass on His words to the congregations, but we should not identify them with our modern church leadership structures. Ephesus was a hard-working, committed, evangelical church that was undeterred by local opposition. Paul had warned that the flock would be attacked by purveyors of false doctrine. The Ephesian leaders had heeded the prophecy and seen the deceivers off. Little is known of the Nicolaitans except that the word means 'people destroyer'. Commendable as the Ephesians' discernment was, something had gone from the church. They had lost their fervent love for Jesus.

This is serious enough for Jesus to remove a lampstand – to close a church down. Use the Personal Application section to remind your group that dogged faithfulness without love is not Christian faith. Read the Seeing Jesus section. How would your church score if Jesus conducted an OFSTED report on it?

Discussion Starters 1 and 2 invite us to repent. There is no special technique for restoring lost love. It happens as we contemplate how much Jesus loves us.

Busyness can blind us. Jesus can remove a lampstand but a church plough on regardless. Use Discussion Starters 3 and 4 to expose the signs of cold duty and to encourage vigilance, so that we constantly stir up our love for Jesus.

Doctrine is important. Discussion Starters 5 and 6 remind us of the destructive power of error and the need to test truth claims. This is especially needful in an age of global communications. Emphasise the centrality of the Scriptures, properly interpreted, and the lifestyles of the teachers.

Each letter mentions overcomers. They are those who retain their first love. To them Jesus promises paradise – the garden city called New Jerusalem where the tree of life is freely accessible for ever.

Week 2: Smyrna – The Call to Suffer

Icebreaker
The opening icebreaker invites us to look at our lives, our beliefs and our behaviour in the light of our public witness. Are we 'guilty' of being like Jesus?

Aim of the Session
For many Western Christians, persecution happens elsewhere. However, in an increasingly hostile world, many Westerners find themselves in trouble for their faith. The issue for Smyrnian believers concerned who was Lord. A loyal city like Smyrna expected its citizens to pay homage to Caesar as a civic duty. The Christians paid homage to Jesus. 'Jesus is Lord' is always a political statement. It says He is the Caesar, and to Rome that was treason.

Jewish opposition was familiar to the Early Church. For Jews to acknowledge that Jesus was the Messiah was to admit their wrongdoing. Many Jews, like John and Paul, did precisely that, but these Jewish fundamentalists slandered the Christians by suggesting they were a politically subversive group. It led to the persecution that Jesus prophesied.

The true people of God are known by their works. Those that want to kill Christians are of the devil, whatever their racial claims. Remind your group that salvation is by grace, not by race. Whether of Jewish or Gentile background, there is only one way to be saved, and that is through the finished work of Christ. The Smyrnian Christians had lost much for their brave confession, and they were about to lose more. But these 'losers' are actually winners and they will gain the crown of life.

No sane person wants persecution, but we should recall that death of the body is not the end. The Bible teaches a second death. This follows the final judgment when the devil will be cast into the lake of fire, as will all those who chose to be his children. The world may mock the imagery but that does not detract from the reality, or from the fact that Jesus saves us from hell.

It costs to be a follower of Christ. Use the Personal Application to remind your group of this fact and to take courage. The Lord is with us, and those who suffer with Him will reign with Him. Discussion Starter 1 asks why we get persecuted. Outwardly, it may be because of jealousy, because we challenge the values of the world, because we restrain evil – but behind it all lies the devil.

Spiritual warfare is a reality for us all. Using Discussion Starter 2, ask your group how that works out in daily life. What are the battlegrounds, what are the weapons, how do we win? The Personal Application reminds us that it is an honour to serve the Lord and bear the reproach of His name.

This letter exposes persecuting Jews as satanic. That doesn't mean we should be anti-Semitic. Use Discussion Starter 3 to remind folk that Jews need the gospel just like the Gentiles and we should love them just the same.

Use Discussion Starters 4, 5 and 6 and the Seeing Jesus section to encourage spiritual robustness and hope in the light of the resurrection of Christ. Remember, the keys of death and hell are in His hands, not the devil's.

Discussion Starter 7 touches on the reality of being saved from hell. The Bible doesn't pander to our fashion for diluting the gospel. Salvation has eternal consequences. There is a second death for unbelievers. It may be helpful to complete this session by praying for those who are undergoing persecution and praying also that we will have courage to share the gospel with all those of our personal acquaintance.

Week 3: Pergamum – The Call to Truth

Icebreaker
The icebreaker is actually about spiritual health. Most of us have inoculations against killer diseases for the sake of our physical health. This icebreaker asks us to consider immunising ourselves spiritually against the soul sicknesses to which we are particularly vulnerable.

Aim of the Session
Pergamum was an unquestionably dark city. Zeus' great altar, sometimes known as Satan's Seat, was later removed to Nazi Germany by Hitler. Political persecution had led to the martyrdom of Antipas. Yet this church would not be cowed.

Its problem was that of the schizophrenic lifestyle – separating the sacred from the secular. This is a Greek concept, totally removed from a biblical world-view. Numbers 22–25 provides the background for the reference to Balaam. Sexual sin provoked an epidemic that killed thousands. It is very relevant in an age of soaring sexually transmitted diseases.

The Nicolaitans crop up again. Their teaching of 'once saved, always saved, but enjoy the pleasures of the flesh, because it's not what you do but what you believe that counts', sounded plausible and attractive. This antinomian heresy taught that grace releases us from the moral law and favours a permissive lifestyle. It reappeared as situation ethics and is widely believed today. Those who disagree are often classed as legalists. Sadly some are miserable, judgmental, rigid, old-fashioned; such people do not have it right either.

Behaviour is determined by belief. The Personal Application section expresses the truth that we are not freed from sin to do as we please but freed from sin to serve the Lord with gladness. Ensure that all members of your group fully understand this. Use Discussion Starters 1 and 2 to emphasise the importance of sound doctrine as a basis for sound living. The Nicolaitans were deceptive. Using Discussion Starter 3, explore some of the lies of the devil in our contemporary world, eg casual sex is OK provided you use a condom. It's only sex, anyway. It's OK to get drunk provided you don't drive. Discussion Starters 4 and 5 remind us of our responsibility to take the true gospel into a world of deceit where any and all beliefs are considered equally valid.

The Nicolaitans encouraged the practice of eating idolatrous food. Discussion Starter 6 reminds us how important the Word of God is in shaping our beliefs and our identity. The truly faithful will be nourished on the inside. Let's be honest, a life of partying and pleasure-seeking and sexual compromise does not nourish the soul. It does the opposite.

The white stone that Jesus gives to the overcomers is a security pass to the best party of all. It beats a rubber stamp at a Saturday nightclub. Using Discussion Starter 7, remind your group that each one has a personal, precious and unique relationship with Jesus. Some may be unsure about their new name in Christ. In the Bible, your name is your identity, so focus on the quality of relationship that the individuals in your group have with Jesus.

Finally, Jesus will have no nonsense with those who pervert the Christian faith. The two-edged sword is the Roman short sword used lethally for close-quarter fighting. The sword of the Spirit has penetrating power to expose not only error but also the hearts of those who propagate error.

His voice is also the sound of thundering waters; when He speaks, we must listen. Perhaps some in your group need to read the Gospels afresh and to take the words of Jesus seriously. When all the lies and deceits are done, His great voice still resounds throughout the universe.

Week 4: Thyatira – The Call to Holiness

Icebreaker
The opening icebreaker needs a little explanation. A cultural idol may literally be connected to another religion or it may be devotion to a pop group, soap opera, or to a consumer, fashion, political or cult lifestyle. The keyword is devotion.

Aim of the Session
The church in Thyatira was in serious trouble. Although it had grown successfully from its beginnings, a Nicolaitan-type heresy had reached crisis proportions here. Its arch-exponent in the church was a particular woman of bewitching power, codenamed Jezebel. It is unlikely that this was her real name. Jesus is reminding His hearers of the terrible reign of King Ahab over Israel. His wife, Jezebel, was a witch queen, a militant fertility cult devotee

who set about killing God's prophets. She met her match in the prophet Elijah.

The Thyatiran Jezebel had formed her own society within the church to teach a mix of New Age spirituality and Gnostic enlightenment. It drew people who had a fascination for esoteric mysteries. The ultimate initiation took place in the woman's bed in a sacred sex ritual accompanied by eating meat devoted to idols.

Jesus exposes this teaching for what it is – thoroughly satanic. Given the rise of popular paganism in our culture, we need to be aware of the dangers. We cannot mix our faith with earth magic, however beguilingly innocent it may appear. The church leaders should have dealt with this woman. Their failure left the church liable to degenerate into a pagan fertility cult. Jesus won't have that! Since the woman refuses to repent, consistent with biblical teaching, she will pay the price of her sin. She and her followers will suffer sickness, and her children will die. This should be understood literally.

When immorality strikes a church it is tempting to go into extreme self-denial, but Jesus lays no more on them than the apostolic agreement recorded in Acts 15. Use Discussion Starters 1 and 2 to explore the nature of true holiness. The Seeing Jesus section focuses on the Lord blazing with holy fire in the midst of His churches. Holiness is about transparent integrity before Him.

The world is full of secret societies, inner circles and government secrets, but Jesus is the Lord and He knows them all. He, and those who refuse the blandishments of sin, will rule the nations in fulfilment of Psalm 2. Explore this using Discussion Starter 3.

In a perverse and adulterous generation, the Jezebel spirit can appear in any church. Use Discussion Starter 4 not as a weapon against feminism or women's ministry but to identify the dangers of novel 'spiritual' teaching infiltrating a church through seductive personalities.

Discussion Starter 5 focuses on one particularly widespread problem in the Church at present. Discussion Starter 6 needs careful handling. The connection between sickness and sin is generally direct, eg promiscuous sex leads to sexually transmitted diseases, alcoholism leads to liver problems. However, we must not equate all sickness with sin.

The planet Venus, known as the morning star, is in honour of the seductive sex goddess. Jesus claims the morning star as His own title. Use Discussion Starter 7 to remind people to praise the Lord when they see this star – and to have nothing to do with horoscopes.

The Personal Application is there to simplify the battlefield for those who find it all rather confusing. Encourage your group to know that God has provided all the resources necessary for us to overcome the world's corruption. Stir them to be strong, to live in the light, to hold on to sound doctrine, and by His grace to be spiritual victors.

Week 5: Sardis – The Call to Life

Icebreaker
People talk about spirituality today but that does not necessarily equate with spiritual life. Life comes from the Holy Spirit. The opening icebreaker gives an opportunity for members of your group to talk about their own authentic experiences of the Holy Spirit, both past and present.

Aim of the Session
The Sardis church was elegantly tragic. It had a reputation as a centre of spiritual life but was actually dead. The

church relied upon an illustrious past. It had noble traditions and was well-connected, but the personal faith of the individuals was merely nominal. Given good business management and a modicum of public talent, such churches can get by perfectly well without Jesus!

This church, like an old tree, had died on the inside and didn't know it. Everything done 'decently and in order' doesn't mean it is acceptable before God. Instead of being a powerhouse of the Holy Spirit, this church was a deadly morgue and its atmosphere was toxic. Jesus urges them to wake up before it's too late. They must recapture the old fire. Failing that, Jesus will come like an unwelcome thief to ransack the church of its remaining assets.

It is a reality of life that behind outward, legalistic correctness often lies licentiousness. Mere religion is usually a hypocritical cloak for a corrupt heart – something Jesus exposed in the Pharisees. The fine robes worn in this church were soiled in the eyes of the Lord. These people were not in the Lamb's book of life. Yet some had pure robes; these overcomers kept the living faith and could be assured of eternal life.

We should not set out to be wrongly critical of any church, but we are required to discern. Use Discussion Starters 1 and 2 to examine this vital matter of spiritual life.

This challenging letter reminds us that people can be church members and still go to hell. Use the Personal Application to challenge your group members concerning their experience of the Holy Spirit. Are they truly born again? Are their lives transformed? Are they assured that their names are on the only membership roll that really counts? Discussion Starter 3 will allow you to focus on the issue.

Discussion Starters 4 and 5 enable us think about the Holy Spirit. The seven spirits are not seven different

Holy Spirits, but represent the perfection of His diverse operations in the world. What does the Holy Spirit do in our lives? Explore areas like the fruit of the Spirit, the gifts of the Spirit, praying in the Spirit, the empowering of the Spirit, the comfort of the Spirit, the guidance of the Spirit, the instruction of the Spirit – to name but seven!

Nominal Christianity is less prevalent in Britain than it was. However, it is still possible to find people who attend church but who have no personal encounter with the Lord. They need a touch of the Holy Spirit. Discussion Starter 6 helps us open up how we can help such people have a living encounter with Christ.

Discussion Starter 7 represents a challenge to us all. Complacency is deadly. We must stir up the gift within us. Worship must never become routine. We need holy fire. The Seeing Jesus section reminds us that spiritual life and fire are found in Christ and are ministered into our lives by the Holy Spirit.

The messengers of the churches, likewise, must not depend on education and eloquence. They must proclaim the message under the anointing of the Holy Spirit. Perhaps end this session by praying for a fresh touch of the Holy Spirit on your lives.

Week 6: Philadelphia – The Call to Enter

Icebreaker
In our security-conscious world, proof of identity becomes increasingly necessary. The opening icebreaker sets the scene for a study on identity and rights of access into the kingdom of God.

Aim of the Session

The Philadelphian church was relatively weak. It also
faced considerable opposition from the local Jewish
synagogue. Although this probably involved the same
slander experienced by others, the issue here was more
doctrinal. What right did this church have to claim that it
represented the true people of God? To Jews, the Gentiles
were outside and damnable. Those of their own who
joined the church betrayed their race, their culture and
their religion. They lost all claim to the kingdom of God.

Everything all turns on the identity of Jesus. He is the true
Messiah in spite of the denials of His opponents. Jesus
holds the key of David. This key represents the right of
access into the kingdom of God for all those who confess
Him to be Christ, the Son of God. This is the door that
Jesus has opened and it is open to everyone who calls
on His name, whatever their background. He is also the
spiritual house and those who confess Him are living
stones, pillars inscribed with kingdom identity and bearing
Christ's own signature. Those who try to deny the Church
this privilege are telling lies. They themselves have sold
out to the devil and have lost the right of access to the
kingdom of God.

Is there no hope for the Jews, then? Yes, there is. They,
like the Gentiles, can be saved. They are no more cursed
or damned than anyone else, so they are part of the
mission field. Paul foresaw a day when the nation would
turn back to God. Jesus sets this prior to His second
coming.

Great trials will come upon the world. The structure of
Revelation indicates that believers do not escape this.
Rather, they are kept through it by Christ Himself. They
are not defeated by Satan, and they do not lose faith,
hope and love.

The Seeing Jesus section reminds us of the proofs of Jesus' Messiahship. He qualifies in every way by fulfilling all the Old Testament prophecies. He is also risen from the dead. As such He holds all the keys. Remind people that whatever the trials they face, Jesus will see them through.

The Personal Application reassures us of our future hope. We may feel inadequate in the eyes of the world, or of other religions. People may despise us as pathetic, no-brainers with outmoded beliefs, but that is not the truth. One day we will inherit the crown.

Use Discussion Starters 1 and 2 to explore what it means to enter the kingdom of God. Remember, the Church is not the kingdom of God; it is a representation and instrument of the kingdom.

Discussion Starters 3 and 4 give us an opportunity to examine the Messianic claims of Jesus. Because of misunderstandings about Him, many Jews cannot grasp the fact that Jesus is their legitimate Messiah. The New Testament resolves every one of these misunderstandings. Look at the testimony of His life, the prophetic fulfilment, the fact of His resurrection and the superiority of the new covenant.

The fruit of the kingdom of God is often borne in the storms of life. Discussion Starters 5 to 7 focus on this reality. Trials are proving grounds for the worth of our faith.

You might wish to end this session by thanking God that we are members of His kingdom and praying for the Jewish people.

Week 7: Laodicea – The Call to Authenticity

Icebreaker
Rely on your own taste buds or use a thermometer to serve awful drinks to your group! The point is to help people realise how distasteful lukewarmness is.

Aim of the Session
The Laodicean church was prosperous. Its members were moneyed and they knew how to spend it. Such a wealthy church could enjoy the good life. Well fed, fashionably dressed, educated, widely travelled, these sophisticates didn't even miss the presence of Jesus.

The tale of the emperor's new clothes is about a vain king conned by salesmen into believing he was magnificently dressed in clothes only a king could see. Because he was king, everyone agreed with him, except for one honest child who saw that the king was parading in his birthday suit. What the Laodicean Christians thought made them so fine actually left them looking tragic in the eyes of the Lord. The 'water' this church offered looked promising – until you tasted it. Then you spat it out in disgust.

The proper emphasis here is on authenticity rather than spiritual temperature. The church should deliver what it promises. That's why Jesus said He likes both hot and cold water, but not lukewarm. Laodicea's water supply from Colossae supplied good cold water for drinking. The hot mineral springs in the hills provided a healing spa but by the time it reached Laodicea that water was both undrinkable and too cool for a bath. Lacking authenticity, this prosperous, self-deluding church was neither one thing nor the other. Spiritually, it could neither refresh nor heal. It was truly sickening!

For all their faults, Jesus still loves His church and He urges His people to repent. He is knocking on the door. Forget Holman Hunt's painting, *Light of the World* for a moment. The imagery here is that of a travelling salesman offering better wares than the local suppliers. They could only serve the outward, whereas Jesus provides for the heart. Like the traders in the city He, too, has gold, fine clothes and medicines. The difference is, His will make them truly wealthy, well-clad and healthy.

Consumerism saps spiritual life. Retail therapy leaves people spiritually bankrupt, naked and blind. Obsessions with pension plans can displace the importance of treasure in heaven. Use Discussion Starters 1 and 2 to consider this.

Use Discussion Starter 3 to explore how the Church can recover its relevance to the spiritual longings in society. Discussion Starter 4 provides an opportunity to understand the real needs of people.

Discussion Starter 5 reminds us that the Lord disciplines those He loves but He does so for our blessing and improvement. Use Discussion Starter 6 to examine how we let Jesus in and buy from Him. It involves recognising our tragic condition and changing our buying habits.

Use the Personal Application and Discussion Starter 7 to challenge group members with the call to authenticity. People have a right to expect what we promise. The Church must deliver the goods. It is not enough to offer a place of social respectability for the well heeled. People need the water of life: cool enough to refresh them; hot enough to heal them.

We finish this series with the Seeing Jesus section. He is the Authentic One. The Church may be persecuted, it may face deception, there are those who would seduce it away from Christ, but He remains true. He is the Lord of all creation and the firstborn from the dead; the beginning and the end. You may wish to end this session by taking another look at John's resplendent vision of Christ and then spend some time in worship and thanksgiving.

National Distributors

UK: (and countries not listed below)
CWR, Waverley Abbey House, Waverley Lane, Farnham, Surrey GU9 8EP.
Tel: (01252) 784700 Outside UK (44) 1252 784700

AUSTRALIA: CMC Australasia, PO Box 519, Belmont, Victoria 3216.
Tel: (03) 5241 3288 Fax: (03) 5241 3290

CANADA: David C Cook Distribution Canada, PO Box 98, 55 Woodslee Avenue, Paris, Ontario N3L 3E5.
Tel: 1800 263 2664

GHANA: Challenge Enterprises of Ghana, PO Box 5723, Accra.
Tel: (021) 222437/223249 Fax: (021) 226227

HONG KONG: Cross Communications Ltd, 1/F, 562A Nathan Road, Kowloon.
Tel: 2780 1188 Fax: 2770 6229

INDIA: Crystal Communications, 10-3-18/4/1, East Marredpalli, Secunderabad – 500026, Andhra Pradesh.
Tel/Fax: (040) 27737145

KENYA: Keswick Books and Gifts Ltd, PO Box 10242, Nairobi.
Tel: (02) 331692/226047 Fax: (02) 728557

MALAYSIA: Salvation Book Centre (M) Sdn Bhd, 23 Jalan SS 2/64, 47300 Petaling Jaya, Selangor.
Tel: (03) 78766411/78766797 Fax: (03) 78757066/78756360

NEW ZEALAND: CMC Australasia, PO Box 303298, North Harbour, Auckland 0751.
Tel: 0800 449 408 Fax: 0800 449 049

NIGERIA: FBFM, Helen Baugh House, 96 St Finbarr's College Road, Akoka, Lagos.
Tel: (01) 7747429/4700218/825775/827264

PHILIPPINES: OMF Literature Inc, 776 Boni Avenue, Mandaluyong City.
Tel: (02) 531 2183 Fax: (02) 531 1960

SINGAPORE: Alby Commercial Enterprises Pte Ltd, 95 Kallang Avenue #04-00, AIS Industrial Building,
339420. Tel: (65) 629 27238 Fax: (65) 629 27235

SOUTH AFRICA: Struik Christian Books, 80 MacKenzie Street, PO Box 1144, Cape Town 8000.
Tel: (021) 462 4360 Fax: (021) 461 3612

SRI LANKA: Christombu Publications (Pvt) Ltd, Bartleet House, 65 Braybrooke Place, Colombo 2.
Tel: (9411) 2421073/2447665

TANZANIA: CLC Christian Book Centre, PO Box 1384, Mkwepu Street, Dar es Salaam.
Tel/Fax: (022) 2119439

USA: David C Cook Distribution Canada, PO Box 98, 55 Woodslee Avenue, Paris, Ontario N3L 3E5, Canada.
Tel: 1800 263 2664

ZIMBABWE: Word of Life Books (Pvt) Ltd, Christian Media Centre, 8 Aberdeen Road, Avondale, PO Box
A480 Avondale, Harare.
Tel: (04) 333355 or 091301188

For email addresses, visit the CWR website: www.cwr.org.uk
CWR is a registered charity – Number 294387
CWR is a limited company registered in England – Registration Number 1990308

Our *Cover to Cover* resources enable you to dig deep into God's transforming Word

Empower your prayer life

Discover how the Lord's Prayer – seemingly so simple – encompasses every aspect of prayer and how praying in line with it will give you a more powerful and effective prayer life.

• See God as your loving Father more clearly
• Submit to His will more joyfully
• Increase your joy by forgiving and receiving forgiveness

ISBN: 978-1-85345-460-8
Only £3.99

Do Christ's will in all times and all places

Take an in-depth look at the messages King Jesus sent to seven first-century churches, and learn how to:

• Love Him supremely
• Suffer for His sake joyfully
• Adhere to truth faithfully – and much more

His words are sobering, calling us higher and inviting us to draw fresh grace from the One who 'was and is and is to come'.

ISBN: 978-1-85345-461-5
Only £3.99

Also available in the *Cover to Cover Bible Study* series

1 Corinthians
Growing a Spirit-filled church
ISBN: 978-1-85345-374-8

Ecclesiastes
Hard questions and spiritual answers
ISBN: 978-1-85345-371-7

1 Timothy
Healthy churches – effective Christians
ISBN: 978-1-85345-291-8

Ephesians
Claiming your inheritance
ISBN: 978-1-85345-229-1

2 Timothy and Titus
Vital Christianity
ISBN: 978-1-85345-338-0

Fruit of the Spirit
Growing more like Jesus
ISBN: 978-1-85345-375-5

23rd Psalm
The Lord is my Shepherd
ISBN: 978-1-85345-449-3

Genesis 1–11
Foundations of reality
ISBN: 978-1-85345-404-2

God's Rescue Plan
Finding God's fingerprints on human history
ISBN: 978-1-85345-294-9

Great Prayers of the Bible
Applying them to our lives today
ISBN: 978-1-85345-253-6

Hebrews
Jesus – simply the best
ISBN: 978-1-85345-337-3

Hosea
The love that never fails
ISBN: 978-1-85345-290-1

James
Faith in action
ISBN: 978-1-85345-293-2

Jeremiah
The passionate prophet
ISBN: 978-1-85345-372-4

John's Gospel
Exploring the seven miraculous signs
ISBN: 978-1-85345-295-6

Joseph
The power of forgiveness and reconciliation
ISBN: 978-1-85345-252-9

Mark
Life as it is meant to be lived
ISBN: 978-1-85345-233-8

Moses
Face to face with God
ISBN: 978-1-85345-336-6

Nehemiah
Principles for life
ISBN: 978-1-85345-335-9

Parables
Communicating God on earth
ISBN: 978-1-85345-340-3

Philemon
From slavery to freedom
ISBN: 978-1-85345-453-0

Philippians
Living for the sake of the gospel
ISBN: 978-1-85345-421-9

Proverbs
Living a life of wisdom
ISBN: 978-1-85345-373-1

Revelation 4–22
The Lamb wins! Christ's final victory
ISBN: 978-1-85345-411-0

Rivers of Justice
Responding to God's call to righteousness today
ISBN: 978-1-85345-339-7

Ruth
Loving kindness in action
ISBN: 978-1-85345-231-4

The Covenants
God's promises and their relevance today
ISBN: 978-1-85345-255-0

The Divine Blueprint
God's extraordinary power in ordinary lives
ISBN: 978-1-85345-292-5

The Holy Spirit
Understanding and experiencing Him
ISBN: 978-1-85345-254-3

The Image of God
His attributes and character
ISBN: 978-1-85345-228-4

The Kingdom
Studies from Matthew's Gospel
ISBN: 978-1-85345-251-2

The Letter to the Colossians
In Christ alone
ISBN: 978-1-85345-405-9

The Letter to the Romans
Good news for everyone
ISBN: 978-1-85345-250-5

The Prodigal Son
Amazing grace
ISBN: 978-1-85345-412-7

The Second Coming
Living in the light of Jesus' return
ISBN: 978-1-85345-422-6

The Sermon on the Mount
Life within the new covenant
ISBN: 978-1-85345-370-0

The Tabernacle
Entering into God's presence
ISBN: 978-1-85345-230-7

The Uniqueness of our Faith
What makes Christianity distinctive?
ISBN: 978-1-85345-232-1

£3.99 each (plus p&p)
Prices correct at time of printing

Cover to Cover Every Day
Gain deeper knowledge of the Bible

Our *Cover to Cover Every Day* bimonthly dated notes will take you deep into each book of the Bible over a five-year period.

Each issue features contributions from two different authors and a reflection on a psalm each weekend by Philip Greenslade.

- Covers every book of the Bible in a rolling five-year curriculum
- Daily Scripture readings and a suggested prayer
- Highly respected and well known authors

ISSN: 1744-0114
Only £2.25 each (plus p&p)
£12.50 for annual UK subscription (6 issues)
£12.50 for annual email subscription
(available from www.cwr.org.uk/store)

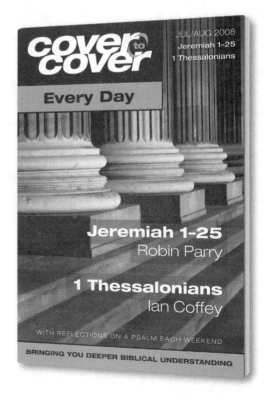